POSTCARD FROM THE SHORE

Other Highland Books

by F.F. Bruce
Paul and His Converts

edited by Christopher Catherwood
Martyn Lloyd-Jones: Chosen by God

edited by Edward England
My Call to Preach
A Way with Words: A Handbook for Christian Writers
David Watson: A Portrait by his Friends

edited by Ann England
We Believe in Healing

by Michael Green
Evangelism in the Early Church

by Michael Harper
Walk in the Spirit

by Benson Idahosa
Power for Your Zero Hour
Faith can Change Your Destiny

by Thomas à Kempis
The Imitation of Christ

by Gordon MacDonald
Ordering Your Private World

by J. Oswald Sanders
Prayer Power Unlimited
What of Those who Have Never Heard?

by Edith Schaeffer
What is a Family?

by John Sherrill
They Speak with Other Tongues

by Jack R. Taylor
The Hallelujah Factor

by Kenneth Taylor
How to Grow – First Steps for New Christians

by Phyllis Thompson
Gladys Aylward: A London Sparrow

by Paul Tournier
A Doctor's Casebook in the Light of the Bible
Learning to Grow Old
Marriage Difficulties
A Place for You
Secrets
The Strong and the Weak

by Sabina Wurmbrand
The Pastor's Wife

Postcard from the Shore

Luci Shaw

HIGHLAND BOOKS

First published in 1985 by Harold Shaw
Publishers, Wheaton, Illinois, U.S.A.

This British edition 1986

Grateful acknowledgement is made to the editors
of the following periodicals, in which some of these
poems first appeared: The Banner, Campus Life, Eternity,
Christianity and Literature, The Cresset, His, Interest,
Partnership, Radix, Time of Singing, Today's Christian
Woman, Wellspring.

Photographs: Marge Gieser, p 58; Luci Shaw, cover,
pp 8, 15, 16, 24, 29, 52, 72, 77, 83; David Singer,
pp 34, 50, 66, 84.

Printed in Great Britain for
HIGHLAND BOOKS
6 The White House, Beacon Road,
Crowborough, East Sussex TN6 1AB
by Richard Clay Ltd
Bungay, Suffolk

to Harold, lover and best friend,

and to David & Karen
Rick & Donna
Jack & Marlene
Pennie & Eric

friends of the heart with whom
we have explored new shorelines

Contents

Horizons

A Fore Word

For those of us who dwell on large land masses, the shore is often the end of a journey, but also a new frontier; it presents a boundary, but a clean view of the horizon as well. The shore was a place where miracles happened in the Bible (baby Moses by the Nile, the crossing of the Red Sea, Jonah vomited by the whale), and Jesus' last miracle—the great draft of fish—was done by Galilee ("It was early morning, and Jesus stood on the shore") followed by a breakfast picnic of fish broiled simply on a small fire, which Jesus shared with his friends after their long night on the lake.

Signs and wonders, moments of perception and delight, pointers that remind me of the Creator and Provider crop up in my journal. The entry for *Monday, February 11, 1985,* reads:

> Each day follows the last with a bright froth curling off its crest, like waves in sequence, the air flowing in from the Gulf freighted with glistening particles of salt, sand, and spray.
>
> Standing here on a beach on Sanibel Island, we find ourselves at the joining of elements—earth, air, water (and the sun adds the fourth—fire). The distances are tremendous; a whole continent stretches itself horizontally away behind us, as does the sea in front of us; the ocean floor plummets from the continental shelf to an invisible depth at our feet, dark blue and mysterious; and the sky without clouds—we can look up and up forever through its light-years of distance. All

these infinities meet and mark us, and dance with each other, on this very spot. The edges shift in and out a bit with winds and tides, but these fundamental borders give us a sense of the universe and the acts of God.

For all of my days, the effortless, random beauty of shells and fish, of stones and sea-birds, has signalled divine generosity, reflected the complexity and variety of God's mind, reminded me of the importance of the microscopic and particulate as well as the vast and collective.

The shore has always been for me one of the informing metaphors of life. As a young teen-ager I wrote "Wave":

I sweep over beaches with shells in my fingers,
I cover the fore-shore with silver-gold sand,
I glaze the bright earth with a crystal that lingers
and scatter foam-lace with a delicate hand.

Like a gull in a windstorm, I fly from mid-ocean.
The tempest behind me, I hammer the ground,
yet I soothe like a mother, with monotone motion
the little, live creatures that in me abound.

I'm a song, I'm a zephyr, the little blue daughter
of my great, blue mother, the overhead sky,
and though I can reign with the proudest of hauteur
I collapse on a beach with a whisper—and die.

In adolescence, waves were my images of both vitality and mortality. The dance of the sea was a living joy, and the shrinking foam of a spent wave taught me something of what yielding and dying must feel like. Yet I knew, both from observation and sensation, that as the salt water sank back from the shore into the ocean it fueled the power of the next wave generation.

J. B. Phillips suggests that the ocean is irresistibly, universally attractive to us because it reminds us of eternity. The multitudinous wrinkling of its surface and the endless arrival of waves show me an ongoing diversity which is never monotonous because God's infinite innovation lies behind it. Each arc of water up the beach, each configuration of shells and stones and dunes and grasses is unique, unrepeatable. A snowflake gives us the usual illustration of one-of-a-kind-ness in any multitude, but shells and waves and sand-grains will do as well.

> *Tuesday, February 12:* I am amazed at how effortlessly I slip into my beachcomber role. As I pad along the shore, eyes scanning the millions of shells in their textured banks, or scattered, embedded in the film of the pulled-back waves, my mind keeps saying to me, "This is pure happiness. This is the state of purest happiness." Bright bits of color catch me in the eye—rosy, rubbery sea-weed, a pearly jingle shell, a ribbed calico cockle patterned in bright tangerine, a live sea-star, a glistening angel-wing—undeserved gifts of Grace winking up at me with the sheen of sun and sea on them, waiting to be fondled with the eye or carried away with me a thousand miles to where they can remind me of these perfect moments. As I bend and lift each one and love it with my touch and glance, I think of how God bent and lifted me, how he chose me and treasures me, how he wants me with him, how singular and precious I must be to him if he came so far to find me.

I find that I cannot choose shells for others nor they for me. The oiled and varnished specimens in gift shops do not attract me. Sometimes, walking the beach, Harold will pick up a shell to give me, but by his choosing of it he has already made it *his.* To me, shells are a parable of personal choice and significance. A volute or a junonia is fascinating enough in itself—with its "folding-out of pink and white, its letting-in of spiral light," but the incident of noticing it in its own setting and taking it for my own renders it notable; its selection is part of its history. Mentally, I see any treasured shell in its original company—an aggregate of shapes and sizes in melon, chestnut, dappled mauve, dawn yellow, dusk, or taupe. We each search out our own colors, our favorite shapes and patterns.

Wednesday, February 13: The wind is gusting to fifty knots today, with huge breakers crashing and throwing up a salt mist, churning the thick layers of shells and making a clinking rustle as the brine sucks down and away through them. After coffee, Harold and I walk the shore with the wind literally pushing us forward, irresistible as the Spirit. Grey, low clouds scud over us at an oblique angle with the sun suddenly breaking through to water the sea's rough silk with milky light. A rim of rain obscures the horizon. All the gulls, terns, plovers, and sanderlings are standing, cowed-looking, on the shore, heads away from the wind, tail feathers ruffled. The rain driving in now, the blast of the weather is invigorating, purgative, healing. C. S. Lewis liked "weather" in any mood. So do I.

Last night after dinner a brilliant sunset poured between the clouds like melted gold. I ran down to the beach to catch it on film before the fire died. There's a splendid satisfaction in knowing that I have a record of this time, this place. I can recall it, courtesy of photographic transparencies and my journal, and in some future moment the visual and verbal impressions will bring back, or call up, the other sense impressions—the spray driven in the singing air, the buffet of wind on the cheekbone, the unceasing sea sounds.

Thursday, February 14: In the aftermath of the storm is its harvest. The waves and their deep turbulence have knocked loose and laid at our feet shells not seen in the earlier, calmer days of this week. Today I have found apple murex, turbans, zebra nerites, distorsios, jewel boxes, tellins, coquinas, spiny oysters, tulips, turnip whelks, moon snails, babies' ears, many of them alive, that is, with their original inhabitant still attached and lively (though in one helmet I found a squatter—a hermit crab which appeared and disappeared inside, quick as a blink). There's a conservationist taboo about collecting "live" shells here on Sanibel; I threw back dozens of them, and several stranded sea-urchins, into the sea. But the empty shells were abundant, and I loaded up a plastic sack and lurched along, barefoot, in and out of waves, with a horde of other collectors avidly searching, bending (it's called the "Sanibel stoop"), raking, and stowing their finds in pails, bags, pockets. The collectors seemed as diverse as the objects of their desire. I saw an ancient bag-lady type calling excitedly, to anyone who would listen, "This is it, kids—the day we've all been waiting for!" and tanned young women in bikinis, oiled to the eyelids, or fathers and kids, or grizzled retirees with their dogs. How does each of them choose what to keep, what to ignore? Are they looking for color, or shape, or species, or size, or rarity, or perfection, or a combination of the above?

Humans aren't the only shell collectors. To the east of our building (we're staying in the condominium of friends), there's a colony of crows in the casuarina trees. (One of them is the only crow I've heard actually saying "Caw," a deliberate and perfectly articulate monosyllable.) Today two of the great, black birds, each with shell in beak, were on the walkway railing while I was shaking sand out of our floor mats. Crows must have a highly developed aesthetic sense; they love to steal and carry shining things like shells and spoons and coins to their nests where they display them with (I think) as much pleasure as we feel when we exhibit art objects or pictures in our homes. In our house there are shells in every room—in old green glass canning jars, in clear lamp bases, on sills, mantels, plaques, mirrors. (I probably overdo two things in the house—the green and the shells, but both inform and delight me.) I have shells piled in ceramic bowls together with slate pebbles, and buttons of driftwood, and agates, and crab carapaces gleaned from beaches around the world.

The beaches! I remember Bondi, in Sydney, where the towering, ceaseless surf leaves you breathless, spent, and exhilarated all at once. Or the miles of level sand at Westward Ho! on England's south coast that invite you to run and never stop. In my mind, I can watch the crowds of carts, animals, people, who use the wide band of beach on the ocean side of Bombay as a highway. Or I can see myself collecting the tiny, brilliant gems of wave-polished glass chips from among the black pebbles on Newport Beach in Rhode Island. How can I forget East Brewster beach on Cape Cod, site of a score of Shaw vacations, where the water at low tides feels as tepid as the air at noon, and all the bay lies still and lazy under the sun?

One of the beach's best gifts to me is solitude; once, on the pebbled shore of Lake Superior near Ontanagon, I spent a whole day alone (by choice) without shoes, jacket, or food, which was both my challenge to the elements and my way of learning to listen to the landscape. And years later, as I walked the reefs of Long Island in the Bahamas, the turquoise sea shimmered at me until it seemed to dissolve in the heat, and the sense of remoteness was so intense that even heaven and earth seemed to lift away and there was only God and me.

This book begins and ends with wedding poems written for friends. One celebrates the beach as a metaphor of marriage, with changing moods and seasons, ebb and flow and gentle tide-play, storms and sudden silences, and underlying all—a foundation of reef and rock. The other narrates a voyage of relationship, an image that persists through a tumultuous courtship all the way to safe harbor—an arrival at commitment. Both reflect my own experience.

And you, as you read, may find in these pages other images to enlarge you and your views of earth and heaven. If not, perhaps you need to spend a summer by the shore, to feel sand between your toes, and salt in your pores, and to recognize God in the shells at your feet, the sun on your skin, and the wind at your back.

Luci Shaw
West Chicago, Illinois

BOUNDARIES

Seeing the shore

Wedding song for Calvin & Deborah

At ebb tide the sands are stretched—
flat, damp, written on with rain, woven
with a warm air from the west. Stitches
from gulls' feet join dunes with sea
as the tide moves in again
and each succeeding wave spells
a new boundary in a sweeping sentence
punctuated with foam. Its drawing back
pulls a silver foil across the slope.
The film flows, thins, clouds
like a breath-touched mirror, sinks
into the body of the shore.

Your marriage is a beach—a spread
of weeds and wet edges and shells
(pink-lipped, unanchored seeds from the
sea-floor, left in the open air at
high tide, like love-notes).
Now let the seasons shift your singing
sands, let the wind lift and level you,
let water—salt, or fresh from the sky—
shape all the grainy contours
of your joining into ribs and rivulets
and pools for snails and
sea anemones. Let the roar and roll
of breakers polish the quartz and agate
in your detritus. Like gulls, move
with the moment; have no fear; the edges
of the earth, the rims of rock are a
foundation under you. You will not
be swept out to sea.

Freezing rain

Most of the things a poet has to say
are tentative, lists of foggy clues
and suppositions—an unattested version
of the way the wind breathes at night,
an essay at atmosphere, predictions
as unreliable as weather forecasts. I stab
at the truth with a pencil, sometimes,
moved too suddenly to words by the shadings
on a cloud, or its shape, shivering
at a hint of thunder (sure that it
means something).

But in the lines set down on paper
all suggestions become categories—
intuition or illusion edited to sound
like logic. Naked ideas turn assertive
in print, sharp, as intricate
as the edges of a woods in winter seen
against a blank sky. The most fluid
of impressions hardens like frozen
rain. A cold front is passing over:
I hazard a guess; you take it
for reality.

to a young woman calligrapher

You are, yourself, a kind
of calligraphy;
every movement you make
writes a message on the air
in perfect and deliberate
strokes. Come to think of it,
your poise, your balance on
the balls of your feet, your
fingers' flare, the lift
of your neck, your hair—
a flowing curve from crown
to waist—the punctuation
of your glance,
all form themselves
into a smoothly-drafted
letter that leaves
the precision of your signature
engraved in our minds
even after you have
signed off.

Announcement

Yes, we have seen the studies, sepia strokes
across yellowed parchment, the fine detail
of hand and breast and the fall of cloth—
Michelangelo, Caravaggio, Titian, El Greco,
Rouault—each complex madonna positioned,
sketched, enlarged, each likeness plotted at last
on canvas, layered with pigment, like the final
draft of a poem after thirty-nine roughs.

But Mary, virgin, had not sittings, no chance
to pose her piety, no novitiate for body or
for heart. The moment was on her unaware:
the Angel in the room, the impossible demand,
the response without reflection. Only one
word of curiosity, echoing Zechariah's *How?*
yet innocently voiced, without request for proof.
The teen head tilted in light, the hand
trembling a little at the throat, the candid
eyes, wide with acquiescence to shame and glory—
"Be it unto me as you have said."

Defect

The flaw is no more
noticeable, even to me,
than a new moth-hole,
or a very small bald spot
in my fabric.

Yet when
I hold the cloth
up to the window,
the sunlight
bleeds through.

. . . but the word of our God
will stand forever (Isa. 40:6–8)

All flesh is grass
and I can feel myself growing
an inch an hour in the dark,
ornamented with a lyric dew
fine as glass beads, my edges
thin as green hair.
All flesh—
and there are seventeen kinds
of us in this one corner of the
hayfield, along with clover,
oxalis, chicory, Wild Wilber—
close enough cousins for a
succulent hay.
Early mornings
we all smell of rain
enough to drown the microscopic
hoppers and lubricate snails
along their glistening paths:
a fine, wet fragrance, but not
so sweet as this evening, after
the noon scythe.
No longer,
now, are the windows of air
hung with our lace, embroidered
with bees. Laid low, we raise
a new incense, and under the brief
stubble, our roots grieve.

Onlookers

"Sickness is a place . . . where there's no company, where nobody can follow."—Flannery O'Connor

Behind our shield of health, each
of us must sense another's anguish
second-hand; we are agnostic
in the face of dying. So Joseph
felt, observer of the push
and splash of birth, and even Mary,
mourner, under the cross's arm.

Only their son, and God's,
in bearing all our griefs
felt them first-hand, climbing
himself our rugged hill of pain.
His nerves, enfleshed, carried
the messages of nails, the tomb's
chill. His ever-open wounds
still blazon back to us the penalty
we never bore, and heaven
gleams for us more real,
crossed with that human blood.

Permanent I.D.

I will not
prevaricate—
Truth will out.
Identity clings
like a skin. Even
at a hundred yards,
without glasses,
I know my sons in any
crowd. Every book
carries with it
the permanent odor of
its ink. The knowing
hound noses out
the track of a missing
child from all the
other spoor
bisecting the field.
Around the sheep meadow
the barbs of fence wire
carry their catch
of fleece, their multiple
clues of wool.

None of us is innocent.
Even a newborn bears
the taint of genes,
the tendency to choler
or caries. Your cheeks
are smooth and tan

(youth can look
the sun in the eye);
mine are creased
with air and time
and tears.

We are all indelibly
marked. It is impossible
to achieve real
anonymity; let that
be a warning:

Each shred of cloth
or paper, each
jeweled fish scale, each
wood splinter, ice crystal,
heart-shaped green
trefoil, spermatozoon,
speaks of itself alone
and will not be silenced.
Thus, a hair
or a smear of blood
may with certainty
be traced
back to its hero
or criminal.

God and the microscope
are not to be deceived,
will never lie. Neither
can I.

Whenever

Whenever a day's plans are aborted (like
this morning, as the blizzard closed in and
tethered us to the kerosene stove) I think
of possibilities that have never come
real—the white oak out front that would
have touched the sky if lightning
hadn't lopped it, last fall's green-blooded
tomatoes nipped by frost, the writer
who might have become my daughter-in-law.
Less obvious are the poems I may never
finish, each a fetus, waiting, wrinkled,
for an image to break the waters.

Today my world is an envelope of snow
without a stamp; like me, it is going
nowhere, caught in the tail of a dream
like the one pinched off last night by a
sudden buffet of north wind. I was
about to fly again. Now I may never know
if I can.

Arrangement in space and time

Spring-cleaning should have
rid me of them. Summer should have
gathered a fresh bunch.
But this armful of autumn
is almost as antique as the pot
that first received it—the mouth
open like an O, like the rough
circle a woman makes with her elbows
to accept a bouquet.

Brittle, the milkweed stalks break
clean as bones and show the same
straw color. Freed from time, no
seasons pump their juices,
extend their shoots an inch an hour
after rain, swell the silver
strands in their pale purses.
Like dust, timelessness gathers
on the pods and the thin, split
blades. Having lost growth,
they have achieved a kind of
immortality, there where they fill
the winter window,
spilling their tarnished silver
and some old gold.

Going to sleep in the country: Brigham Farm

Ten minutes after the light
is out, the silence, deep as the sky
at night, is broken—the dog in
the yard begins a series of howls
at a siren in the valley. My body
is prone but my mind is bolt upright.
Mentally I pace the square room
from bed to corner fireplace, from
uncurtained window to bookcase
where a hundred volumes hold collected
pages and words, the focus of
a chronology of readers. Book titles
pair off with snatches of dinner
conversation. A character from
Dickens starts a new novel in my head.
The wide floor-boards squeak
under the invisibility of waltzing
partners. The treadle of the old
Singer moves to a slippered foot.

Then a beginning of rain surrounds
the room, the house, until its
steady purpose washes out the other
sounds. Like a candle-stump
whose flame is snuffed, my visions
shrink, settle; like its thin
signature of smoke, restlessness
moves away out the door and down
the passage. Body and mind lie down
at last, together in the dark.

Trespassers

The horizon is clear
cut: an apricot silk
stretches over the hills'
dark profile, and now
that the wind has moved on,
a crystal stillness
presses in place
every tree and blade in
the shallow valley
(our eyes are not
strong enough to prove
this, but skin feels
the weight of dusk).
In the oblique light
each leaf is layered,
green as glass, on its
singular stem. The road
moves cleanly, bisecting
the view. Fields obey
their fences; the whole
view waits for us
to make a mistake,
to tear a ragged corner.
We hesitate even
to speak, to smudge
the silence, to move
the air with our breath,
to disturb sod or stone
with a single step.

Equilibrium

The day balances itself
on the tops of the oak trees.
This morning is as unique
as all the others—the changing
configurations of clouds
to the east, the intensities
of light, the layerings of leaves,
the grass—jewelled with
a heavier dew than yesterday.
Tomorrow the same sun will shine
through the drops and the same
brindled dog will bark at a
passing car, bounding and
scattering moisture, leaving
a new trail, damp and dark
green, across the front yard.

The day moves on, steadies
itself on its foundations.
Like God, true to his own
presuppositions, it shows its
shape at all its edges. As
I walk at noon, my early shadow,
shortened, meets me again
at alternate heels, precisely,
at a calculable angle.
The driveway is washed with sun;
its gravel shines
like gold nuggets.

I bring to each day my own
inconsistency, but in the end,
predictability binds me
more strongly than change—
the resurgence of spring,

the inevitability of weeds, grass
growing back behind the
lawn-mower, the prevalence
of wind, the probability of
evening, the entropy observed
in the age-spots
on the backs of my hands.

The profligate

Conscientious in her stewardship of money,
Miss Prism cut out her new tweed suit last week—
of pure wool fabric, reduced in price for Spring
sewing, a charming, muted rose with flecks of grey
and plum. After the stainless steel pins and the
dressmaker's shears had done their sharp work,
she peeled the seven double shapes up from
the cutting board (each with its tissue twin, like
layers of skin) and approached her high altar,
the old Singer against the wall, with this,
her Lenten oblation. The left-over pieces,
perimeters of precision, she left discarded on the rug,
their weave still taut and true, their color
richly delicate. The cloth's true woollen feel
is a memory of the fields of sheep—fleeces
scoured by rain—of sweat in the shearing sheds,
of the long combing and carding and spinning
of harsh virgin fibers, of dye, darkly boiling,
soaking to the heart of the yarn, of looms
clacking and shaking, the shuttles darting between
stretched skeins. Now, at last, it has all come
to this small untidiness on the sewing-room floor.

And on Easter Sunday, Miss Prism, wearing her new
pink suit with bone buttons, a silk blouse, and
her mother's real pearl earrings, deposits
a solitary dollar in the plate for the needy.

Saved by optics*

First, you must find a chip
   of cold

that has always wanted to see,
to channel the light.
Then, with hands devoid
   of electricity,

without matches even,
and with only splinters
   of strength left,

you must carve it out—the rough
eyeball—from under the brow
   of this ice continent

and polish it between
your curved palms' last warmth
into the double convex
   of a lens,

a gem without frost or crack,
cleansed by the flow
   of its own tears.

Next, you must wait, shivering,
for the slow sun
to reach the zenith
   of his readiness

to work with you. *Now.*
Focused in the eye
   of ice

(angle it exactly,
though its chill finds each
   of your fingers' bones)

a matchless flame collects
until the concentrated scrutiny
   of light

reads the dry tinder into
a saving kindling—ice's gift
   of heat and paradox.

**In* The Desert of Ice, *Jules Verne tells of Arctic explorers, shipwrecked without flame or flint, who kindled a fire by focussing sunlight onto tinder through a lens of ice.*

Letter-press: a proof-reader's complaint

The feet of my mind run to and fro
among the stalks and stems of print,
blistered with words. Letters
are like little knives—I am raw
with the evidence. The crossings of
*t*s, the whipping tails of *g*s, the dots
slung by *i*s, and *j*s, all bombard me
like bullets. Serifs pierce.
Punctuation lacerates: commas flip up
and gouge, brackets staple [sharply]
flesh to paper, an asterisk* pricks like
a burr. And the fangs of "double quotes,"
the skewers of exclamation! Periods,
like pebbles, trip me abruptly. Or else
I slide along the fine, slippery gravel
of ellipses . . . Running such a literal
gauntlet, by the end of a chapter
I feel I may crumple in the gutter,
my wounds blotting the words, bleeding
across the narrow margins, my skin
blanched white as the sheets of paper.

**a star-shaped figure used in printing to indicate a reference to a footnote.*

Split screen: Naples, Florida

From the morning porch I watch the beach with clouds
through bifocals. Like an aging prophet whose vision
calls for double fulfilment—soon, and later—
my sight splits laterally. At upper level people move
along the flat waves' margin in ones and twos, bright
in their flowered swim suits and turquoise walking
shorts. Clearly transient, they are like the terns,
like the tide, moving in and out of sight. The bottom
half of the view, immediate, closer than comfort,
holds the things that must be dealt with—the peeling
paint of the railing, the clutter on the glass
table (half a danish, manuscripts, coffee mugs, books
to be read/reviewed, a sweater's half-knit sleeve,
yesterday's paper.)
I move my head.
Reality is re-defined and still disjunctive.
The sun moves inexorably into my shade and, through
my glasses' curved crystal, finally catches me
in the eye.

Palindrome

Man values God
(if gifts are signs)
and strength of claims
proves words as truth.
But truth as words
proves claims of strength
and signs are gifts
if God values man.

Spice

"Despite the Queen's and Prince Phillip's many differences (he's not keen on corgis or horse-racing, he's impatient and controversial, she can be stubborn, prim, and dictatorial) the marriage is a good one."—Good Housekeeping

Sentimentalists, purists, and some
preachers, advocate marital absolutes—
stability, a clear hierarchy for
decision, a predictable union,
unflawed as a blank page. No wonder
it ends up flat. A truer wedding's
grounded in paradox, answers the pull
of the particular, grapples a score
of rugged issues. Like horned toads
in Eden, incongruities add surprise
to a complacent landscape.

Thank heaven you're romantic and
irascible, I'm opinionated in my
impulsiveness. Thank God we can
lean together in our failing—a rusty
trellis propping a thorned rose.

The separation

No matter how intense
our touching,
or how tender—heads
burrowing fiercely
into chests, or fingers
sure, silken—
there are no
contiguous nerves
to bridge
our bodies' gaps, no
paths of words
to join our souls.
Though each images
the other's pain or
pleasure, two
remain two.
We have been seamed,
not grafted. Though
our steps interlock,
each dances
his own dance.

Do you read into this
a strategy:
separation for
survival's sake?
See it, rather,
as predicament—
our world's ache
to be joined,
to know
and be known.

The comforting

(to Maxine Hancock)

She said she heard the sound
for the first time
that evening

They were walking the back pasture
to river-edge
not talking, taking in
the half-moon, breathing the
lucid silence, when at their left
a wind seemed to lift and he said
"listen" and "there they are"

And she saw that the wind-sound
was wing-sound, that a cloud of ducks
was moving the sky. Without
a cry the pulse of two hundred
feathered wings
shook the whole night

She knew then
how the Comforter had sounded—
the strong breath of his arrival,
the Spirit wing-beat
filling their ears

And knowing our need of comfort
in a dark, chill night
she folded the sound into words
in a little card
and sent it to us with her love

Faith

Spring is a promise
in the closed fist
of a long winter. All
we have got is a raw
slant of light at a low
angle, a rising river
of wind, and an icy rain
that drowns out green
in a tide of mud. It is
the daily postponement
that disillusions. (Once
again the performance
has been cancelled by
the management.) We live
on legends of old
springs. Each evening
brings only remote
possibilities of
renewal: "Maybe
tomorrow." But the
evening and the morning
are the umpteenth day
and the God of sunlit
Eden still looks
on the weather
and calls it good.

Some Christmas stars

Blazes the star behind the hill.
Snow stars glint from the wooden sill.
A spider spins her silver still

within Your darkened stable shed:
in asterisks her webs are spread
to ornament your manger bed.

Where does a spider find the skill
to sew a star? Invisible,
obedient, she works Your will

with her swift silences of thread.
I weave star-poems in my head;
the spider, wordless, spins instead.

Poetry's permanence: the Psalms

David, warrior-king of Israel,
the blood of battle disqualified you
as a temple-builder,
and your dreams and plans
of cedar and stone, hewn for
the house of your God,
were disallowed.

Yet you raised cathedrals
of high praise, tabernacles for
Jehovah's presence, dwellings
for your heaven-ward thoughts, and ours,
that have stood, intricate and
strong, through all our centuries.

Lyrics for Holy Week

1

What was the purchase price of love?
Alabaster and spilled perfume,
thirty pieces of silver spent,
the secret meal in the upper room,
the shallow promise, the hollow kiss,
false witness, a three-year friendship torn,
curses and fears and bitter tears
at the piercing cry of the cock at dawn.

2

Paradox paved his uphill path to death:
his body flogged, then robed in royal red—
his kingship signalled by a crowning wreath
whose thorns grew blooms of blood around his head—
the guiltless God destined for crucifixion—
the shepherd bound, helpless as any lamb
prepared for Passover—and final contradiction,
the blameless one condemned to take our blame.

Highway song for February 14

"Kim I love you—Danny" (roadside graffito)

On overhead and underpass,
beside the road, beyond the grass,

in aerosol or paint or chalk
the stones cry out, the billboards talk.

On rock and wall and bridge and tree,
boldly engraved for all to see,

hearts and initials intertwine
their passionate, short-lived valentine.

I'm listening for a longer Lover
whose declaration lasts forever:

from field and flower, through wind and breath,
in straw and star, by birth and death,

his urgent language of desire
flickers in dew and frost and fire.

This earliest spring that I have seen
shows me his tender love in green,

and on my windshield, clear and plain,
my Dearest signs his name in rain.

H O R I Z O N S

Mixed media

Eleuthera ("Freedom"), Bahamas

Finned, masked, body bright as a bone under
water, traced with tricks of waves' edges,
I have left land to shift into new gear. It is
like flying—weightless, floating. Thighs
slick as a seal's sides, I fluke through
colored schools of scales that turn at a flick,
glint past my foreign cheek. Or I can hang
motionless in the caves of light, clear as air.
My hands, down-branched like sea-stalks, touch
at a coral's rasp, and the pink weeds' slip
and frill.

Having swum like a gull I long now
to crease the sea's skin, to break water,
to rise airborne, to fly, gliding easy as a fish,
to clothe bird bones, wings angled
flat as planes, plucked high, dripping,
by the lift of feathers, the balance of beak
and body, the up-trusting eye—Oh,
to be at home in the sea, and as clean
and careless, there in the fathomless sky!

Epignosis

I think to myself the name
of the bird on the front lawn—
robin—wondering how
I can hear so well in my head
the name he doesn't know
himself. Nor does he have
a word for sod, or worm, or tree
or light, yet without names
he knows each better than I
for what it is:

sod
for its solidity and spring
under the trident feet,
the smell of the green tangle,
the whispers to the cocked ear
of a thousand roots spreading,
or crawlers in their blind
under-tunnelling;

worm
for the long, thrilling, elastic
pull from the earth after rain,
the wriggle, the luscious
roundness in the throat;

tree
for the swell of buds as the sap
hums up its height, the launch
of its highest branches
onto the planes of air;

light
for its slow warmth, its lift
and beckon into the sun's eye,
where words evaporate
and no names are needed.

Aurora borealis

Those leopards of the sky
whose silver eyes are stars,
they prowl and hunt and crouch and cry
among the purple bars.

The arch of heaven gleams
with paw-prints, gold and grey—
their tracks, their incandescent dreams,
the traces of their prey.

From inter-stellar space
these predators of night
slink off with pale, penumbral grace
and vanish with the light.

postcard from the shore

in a wide cloud, suddenly,
a thousand gulls lift
off the salt lagoon
into a corona
around the sun
                                        they circle
the slopes of air together,
moving so easily, cleanly,
my sand-clogged ankles
ache to run
                              I am trying, now,
to tell you what it is like
but words can only
hint at this moment of
heart's dance, the wonder
of wings, the folly
of flight
                    you would have
to be with me, our heads
thrown back, our eyes full
of flashing feathers, our
eardrums pierced
with splinters of gull sound,
with audible light

Two haiku

1. Night driving

Tranquil, stars pool in
the glass, until a sharp right
spins the universe

2. Telephone lines

Fall's fetishes—bird-
beads of obsidian strung
across the sky's throat

Summer road remembered

head low, tongue
flagging the noon air, regular
pads reprinting
the old pattern
heading north
a trotting dog rises to mind
to signal the hot stretch
between Beloit and Madison

on the shoulder of the road
there is gravel
and a flourish of cow parsley
but mostly I see the steady
dog trot
and the corners of the mouth
pulled back for water

A feathered carol

Between fence posts the five strands of wire are strung with

twenty black birds—nervous quarter-notes perched on a musical

staff—a measure of sparrows—a score to serenade the season—

a treble *obbligato*—a feathered carol marked *tutti, con anime,*

presto agitato, crescendo—until the sudden *finale* of wings . . .

Note

how the hidden bird
resists translation.
Her *droo, droo,* is all
I know of her,
idiosyncratic, purling
from her secret branch
layered behind leaves
and fog. *I am myself,*
the pale treble insists;
I will not be drawn
into your dream.

I sit on the back porch
a long time, wooing,
winding in the sound,
listening upwards for
the meaning of doves or a
clue to clear the air
between us, before
I notice one feather
resting
on the wood step.

The collector

In our house, the first of January
heralds a resolute simplicity. No,
not just the clean calendar on the
kitchen door, nor the new date
on letters; not even the bundling out
of the dry tree with its trail
of needles to the back porch,
but a return to routine. Clearing
the Christmas clutter
signals renewal, a re-ordering;
it is a woman taking off jewelry
before scrubbing the kitchen floor.

And so I lift away the mantel's
necklace, a cedar swag pointed with
blue berries and white lights.
Down comes the rosy ribbon from
the decoy duck's neck, the holly sprig
from the antique scale (my husband
was weighed on it when he was born),
the scarlet candles, riskily lop-
sided from all December's burnings.

For myself, and for this shelf
across the fire-place brick,
I plan a chasteness free of dust
and trivia—a candle-stick or two,
a copper bowl, paired pottery crocks
to anchor arcs of bittersweet.
But with a barely noticed stealth
the wooden width accumulates
its own decor: a spindrift of screws,
shipping labels, old lists,

a brass bell turned silent—its
clapper tongue plucked out by
the root, a pulled wishbone,
a curious knot of wood, an envelope
scribbled with verse, and in April,
part of a robin's egg chipped
from the sky. Disorder spreads
so surely along the mantelpiece
that by early June I feel as though
the only things I've failed
to keep there are
my New Year's resolutions.

Young woman: India, 1982

Street-sung,
the bright vowels
belled from her,
plangent, sharp
as incense,
brassy as the heat
at noon in Bombay.

I turned to catch
her sound
heard quick
as the shape
of a bird is seen
past an open doorway.

Hours later
I am listening, still,
for the edges of
colored
wing feathers.

Into orbit

for Doug Engle

Eyes wise behind their rims,
shoe-laces flying, our eight-year-old
visitor has escaped the house.
We tell him the swing was put up
wrong—the ropes not allowed to hang
loose before we knotted them
to the high branch, so that the two
descenders twist always to a
triangle, its bottom held open
by the wooden slat. He unwinds it,
seats himself, and pumps into a wide
ellipse that veers, throws him off-
balance against the trunk. Curious
still in spite of bruises, he leaps
down, counter-spins the darn thing,
and spread-eagles on the grass
underneath, watching upwards as it
careens and stops and ties itself
again into a spiral tight as DNA,
tenacious as original sin.
                                        In the
swing's circling, can he see the turn,
the inward pull of self's
dark gravity, the need to push
free, fly the wind, fling out beyond
release, find his own trajectory
in an expanding universe?

April

The air is filled with south—
Breath which though soft, unseen,
Pants warm from some far tropic mouth
And mists the world with green.

Military Cemetery: Waterbury, Connecticut

Driving—Chicago to Cape Cod
and back—twice in the same season
I see again the cemetery whose shape
had sowed itself two springs ago
into my furrow mind, when in all those

April woods life lay coiled—waiting,
sun-touched, the earth dreaming dandelions
already, the blood beating green under its
thawed skin. How like a flag the graveyard
drapes the hill. It patterns the slope

with rows of white. The stones stand
like winter stubble, year to year,
like ranks of weathered fingers
marking well the root crop underneath,
the bodies angled behind the steep sod,

ready to rise at a blink of the sun's
eyelid, or any sudden trumpet. Glimpsing
again the ancient burial ground
at sixty miles an hour is a summons
of sorts, a reminder of Joseph's bones:

as once they called a whole nation
out of Egypt into a promised land, so now
these hidden sleepers quicken old images,
long-dormant, brain-buried,
into a new growth, a sprouting of stanzas.

skipping stones

the words are rounded,
well-worn as shore stones—
quartz and granite and
slate smooth as an egg

my ear fingers them
until they fling and scatter
from my mind's tongue,
skipping stones
glancing in the watered
light, touching the tops
of the ribbed ripples
before they sink, singing,
pure and heavy and
true as a plumb
down to their bottoming–
out, the finding of
their final place among
the others lying along
the sea-floor of this page

The Omnipresence

Reminders flicker at us from
odd angles, nor will he be ignored;
we sight him in unlikely places,
oaths and dates and empty tombs.
God. His print is everywhere,
stamped on the macro- and the microcosm.
Feathers, shells, stars, cells speak
his diversity. The multiplicity of
leaf and light says God. Wind,
sensed but unseen, breathes the old
metaphor again. Seasons are his
signature. The double helix
spells his spiral name.
Faith summons him, and doubt
blows only the sheerest skein
of mist across his face.

Prodigality

"Look at the lilies, they neither
work nor weave . . ."—Jesus

The lazy lilies, blooming over there,
wasting their sweetness on the summer air
lend me a metaphor, and certify that I
may waste my wanton praising on the sky.

Bird's eye view

It may take more than one
swallow to make a summer,
but this late day in March
one sightseer robin
makes spring for me.
In a paradox of snow
he listens for worms, and
hearing one—his head a sharp
tilt, his russet breast
warm against white—he intuits
that the hidden crawler
is no longer dormant,
that the cold is only
frosting on a rich earth
moist and chocolate,
full of nuts and seeds
ready to split and flicker
into green, once the sun
has licked the icing off.

Not knowing about
cell division, annelids,
photosynthesis, or the vernal
equinox, (hatched just
last spring he has been
a tourist most of the year)
this rank newcomer
has become my teacher.

Clean slate

My heart's a cove
curved to the sea's
margin. Along
the tide line
particles gleam,
randomly settled by
a sudden sigh
of salt air,
the shifting weight
of a shell.
I am swept clean, ready
to be written on
by rain, or gull's claws,
or the fingers of
waves breaking.

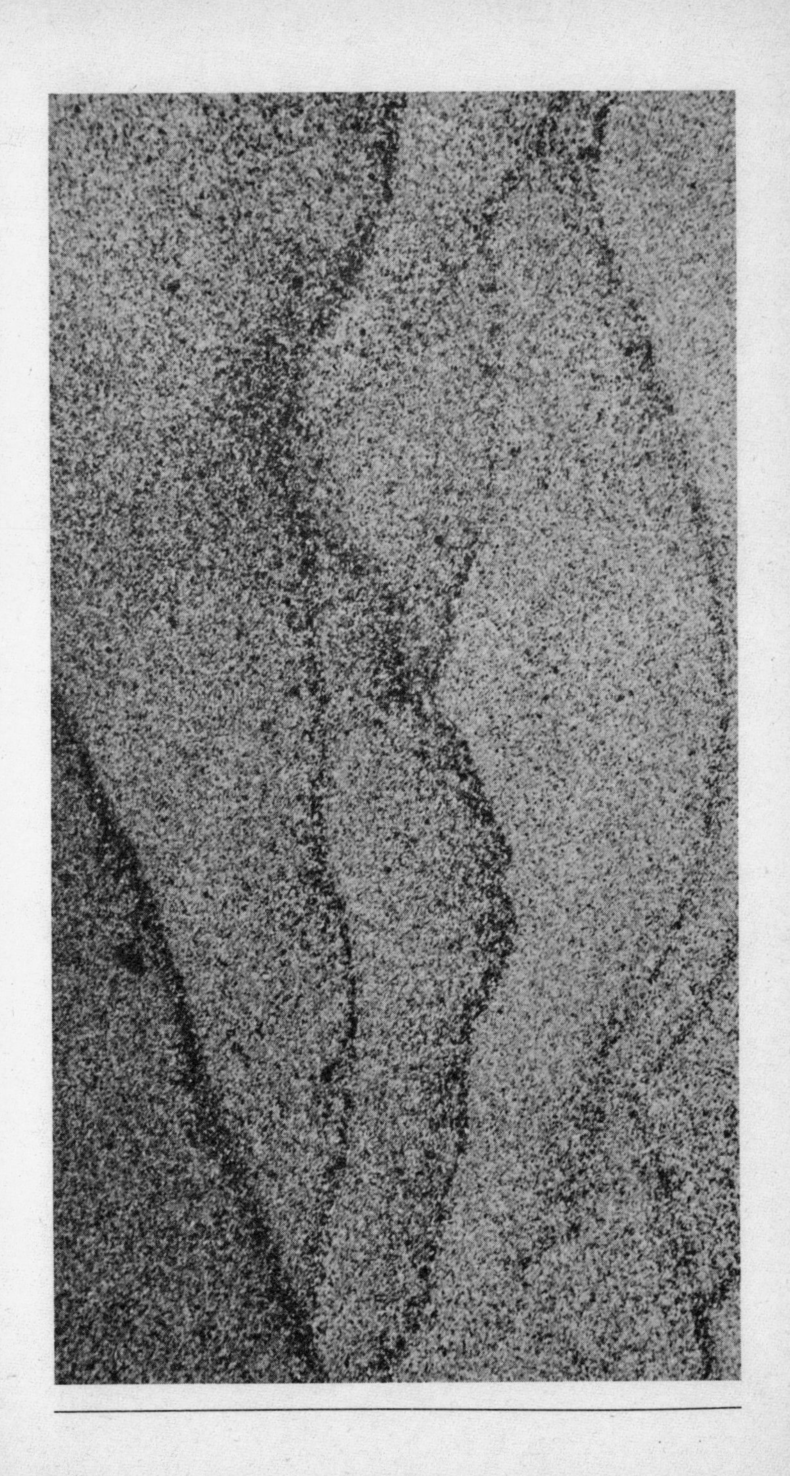

View from the air: North Atlantic, May 1984

It is a long melting, the edges
all blinking and glinting, sputtering
at each small insult, each slap
of waves newly-released themselves
from old borders of ice. Like razors
slicing under from upper atmospheres,
like vapor from an archangel's mouth,
like sharp dreams, like snowy vomit,
like bleached underclothes set out
on the grass to dry, like echoes
of clouds, the ice fields swim,
drifting south, drowning steadily
toward their tropic metamorphosis.

Trauma Center

It was never meant
to burst from the body
so fiercely, to pour
unchannelled from
the five wounds
and the unbandaged brow,
drowning the dark wood,
staining the stones
and the gravel below,
clotting in the air
dark with God's absence.

It was created for
a closed system—
the unbroken
rhythms of human blood
binding the body
of God, circulating
hot, brilliant,
saline, without
interruption
between heart, lungs
and all cells.

But because he
was once emptied
I am each day refilled;
my spirit-arteries
pulse with the vital red
of love; poured out,
it is his life
that now pumps through
my own heart's core.
He bled, and died, and I
have been transfused.

The unveiling

It was God's breath, blowing across
the earth's face, that first polished
the hills with wind, fired them in
the kiln of sun, exposed their
glistening flanks through scarves
of rain. Sky pointers, daily
they balanced glory on their peaks
and plateaus.
Often, afterwards,
Yahweh touched the mountain tops with
meaning: unfurling his iridescence
over Ararat and the emptied ark,
igniting a bush with holiness on Sinai,
etching there, on two stones, his eternal
standards (destined for breaking),
flaming in Moses' eyes as he squinted
against Light, planting balm
even on the battle-bloodied sides
of Gilead. Yes, and on Carmel, the Lord
kindled Elijah's soaked sacrifice to fire
and then reversed himself, his hand
like a cloud opening, pouring on
the febrile, fainting prophet the torrents
that ended more than one drought.
Yahweh
did his best business on the heights:
protecting with his zeal the ark of
covenant from Uzzah's brashness
on Moriah, blessing Obed-Edom there
for the same ark's seclusion in his
threshing yard, then raising on that very rock
his own House—hewn stone and cypress
wood lit with gold, traced with angels,
palms, pomegranates—for beauty and

for glory—the terror of his Presence
curtained with brilliant linen. It was on
Moriah that a son had once been saved
from slaughter as the Lord's young ram,
seen white through its tissue of
thickets, rescued Isaac for his father's
faith.

Time and the Spirit lift for us
the last veil, join in one the holy
double image, focus our seeing on
slain Son/sacrificial Lamb (displayed now
as a whole world's ransom) on the one
out-thrusting rind of rock—Moriah,
Zion, Golgotha, Skull Hill—showplace
for God at work.

"On Mount Zion will the Lord remove the veil that is spread over all nations." Isa. 25:7

"When they came to the place called the Skull, there they crucified him . . . and the curtain of the temple was torn in two." Luke 23:33, 45

"Whenever anyone turns to the Lord, the veil is taken away." 2 Cor. 3:16

The sign of the starfish: Old Lyme, Connecticut

for Paula D'Arcy

With a clutch of debris from the sea
in my hand, wetly translucent quartzes
the shapes of babies' ears,
weather-worn buttons of wood—
I was treading the narrow band
of the beach between waves and sand
when I picked up a starfish. The spell
of the sea and the sky caught suddenly,
and I wondered how we can say
for sure that some galaxy
of sea stars isn't shining
up from an uncharted ocean floor,
or that gulls never fly
the submarine blue as if it were air,
or that fish are not darting somewhere
through the Milky Way
past layers of barnacles lining
the rocks at the outer limits of sky,
or that clusters of oysters
and pearls and sand-dollars
aren't lying, tide-stranded
waiting for light-years to be found
as if Someone had handed
his secret sea-treasures around
on some of the shoals of heaven
as well as here, for me, today,
on a shore in Long Island Sound?

The sounding: Snakeshead Lake

Sun skins the morning lake—
a dream, a dazzle I cannot
pierce. It profiles the dark
movers on the surface—the striders,
snakesheads, water spiders—
the beetles, leaves, loons,
with all their clicks, calls—
the beavers, the strict spears
of the reeds.

The water sleeps, waiting
for me to find my balance on
the floating log. I turn, then,
sun at my back, and probe
the milky shape of my own shadow,
sending my senses diving,
sounding the deep home of
the gilled, gilded, finned,
flaming blue-green, evercool,
underworld water-breathers.

How they hang speechless
in their own element, like bees
in amber. They are caught,
like me, in the wet gap
between bank and bank, air
and earth, linking last winter
and the next, targets
of the sun's swords, the arrows
of the eyes, as Snakeshead Lake
and I, multi-levelled,
wait for a new fathoming.

With Jacob

inexorably I cry
as I wrestle
for the blessing,
thirsty, straining
for the joining
till my desert throat
runs dry.
I must risk
the shrunken sinew
and the laming of
his naming
till I find
my final quenching
in the hollow
of the thigh.

Disciple

Luke 9:57–58

Foxes lope home at dusk, each
to his sure burrow. Every bird
flies the twilight
to her down-lined nest.
Yet come with me to learn
a stern new comfort: the earth's
bed, me on guard at your side,
and, like pilgrim Jacob,
a stone for a pillow.

eucharist

grain cracked
ground   baked
fingered to fragments

        grapes crushed
        casked   splashed
        along tongue

                both tasted
                throat-taken
                gut-gained

blest body
of bread   beaten
to new seed

        joyous juice
        spilled by
        swift spear

                find now fresh
                furrow   harrow
                my fallow heart

At the Church of the Saviour, Washington, D.C.
Summer, 1983

Leaving outside all heat, and the confusion
of self-consciousness, as my own heart's latch
lifts, I enter the door to God's house. The inside
air, cool, blossoms with the scent of multiple
flower heads, and the color.

I find a seat in the circles of others.
As our glances meet, Christ looks out from
the brown eyes and the blue. His presence presses
lightly on us all, each, the unseen hand
moving in blessing from head to head.

Against the wall candles cluster—a benediction of
brown, cream, cinnamon, white—their flames
in the breath-currents moving toward each other
like tongues of fire, like fingers.
In a back row a child makes a soft sound.

A cross unites the space, its arms embracing our
diversity, its shaft both pointing up and reaching
down. As the Word comes incarnate, spoken, broken
once again, love rises in a silent incense, in a unison
of silver sound, from four-score hearts and throats.

With Lindsay: watching sunrise over Stewart Mountain

In my heart I see her climbing down from the loft in her
blue robe, clumsy with sleep. Together we stand in
the cold doorway for first light to embrace us, and in my
pocket her small fingers fold themselves into mine.

Time has set it firm and clear in me, not with a
shutter click, but gently as pectin suspends lemon
slivers: the sun mouthing the lip of the peak,
the spikes of pines dissolving in the glare, the dozing
valley shadowed under its sheet of mist. Dawn's
landscape is finished with two invisible roosters, their
antiphons cleaving the vapor between barn and hen-house.

Today the whole meadow is soaked with gold, the fowls
are silent. Lindsay's glance dances back to me along
the seasons. Though under the passages of sun the child
has grown, the barn has weathered, the shingled roof
shows a new crop of stag-moss, all the drifting, lifting
fogs of the Northwest have left no imprint on this
crystal air. The rising sun runs faster than my calculation,
but I know that each lengthening blade of grass, each
weed head is flamed singularly, like a child waking to light.

Three-year-old

Lauren, toe stubbed,
limps sobbing up the stairs,
clings to my knee

Hugging, I lift her to my hip,
my shoulder, till she's high in my hands
as the fork of a tree

Pain gone like a bad past, she begins
to beat a song on my head with her fingers—
"Zacchaeus was a wee

little man . . ." she sings, and each
winged note falls in its golden spin
like a sycamore key

Home movie

As we drive East the landscape
develops like a film: seamless prairies
give way to a narrative of forests
spliced with plots of hops and potatoes.
The horizon exposes itself in a suspense
of green crests. Incidental rivers
and other bodies of water unroll
into one—vast, salt, smelling of fish.

Two weeks later, the trip home from the
shore runs the whole vacation backwards:
lobster pots vanish, sand falls from
our shoes, a lost beach towel reappears
like a special effect, the scenery
relaxes into flatness. What if our lives
could be unreeled? Our journey taken over?

Landfall

for Ann & John Gordon

It was evening when we first caught sight
of the low, silent sea-coast—our ship
still pitching in swells rough
with memories of the storm, though by then

the air had died to a breath and a sigh,
and the sky was glowing, cloud-innocent,
smooth as the inside of a shell.
What a time it took us, though—what

alternations of tides and what careful
study of charts all through the night
before we could find the narrow break
in the reef. Finally, at dawn, we let

the rise of the incoming tide lift
us through. Beaches glinted in and out
of the salt fog. Whales, curious, blew
as they sighted us. Gulls urged us on

in their imperious way. The cross-
currents, the barnacled black rocks,
levelled a thousand threats at us
between the crests of the breakers,

before the inlet, visible from only one
angle, revealed itself. Sliding behind
a finger of sand that thickened into hand,
arm, elbow, shoulder, we dropped anchor

at last in the bosom of the cove. There
in that calm enclave, we splashed through
shallows to shore to drink deep of spring
water, the relief of arrival, the bliss

of dry sand under our sodden feet. Later,
circled by the land's embrace, we bedded down
on fixed earth and watched, without fear,
the star voyagers circling their own dark ocean.

Nowadays, along that same shore,
beach houses cluster, and a town behind them.
But some early mornings, when the fog
moves in and lays her wedding veil

along the sand, smoothing the sea flat
with its pale film, we can imagine the place
pure, unexplored, virgin, and begin
to discover it all over again.